AF349111

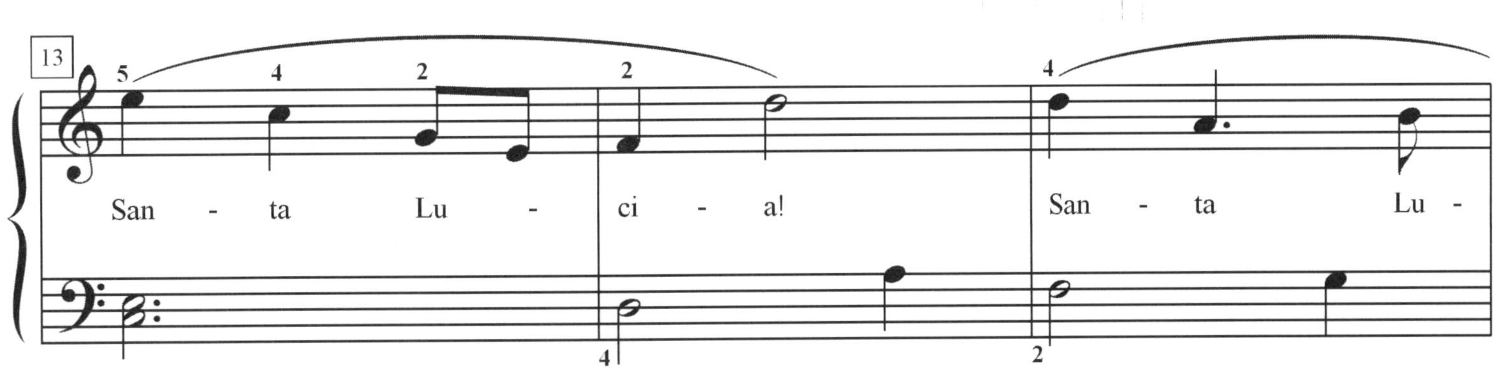

13
5 4 2 2 4
San - ta Lu - ci - a! San - ta Lu -
4 2

16
5
ci - a! Home of fair po - et - ry,
mf
3 2

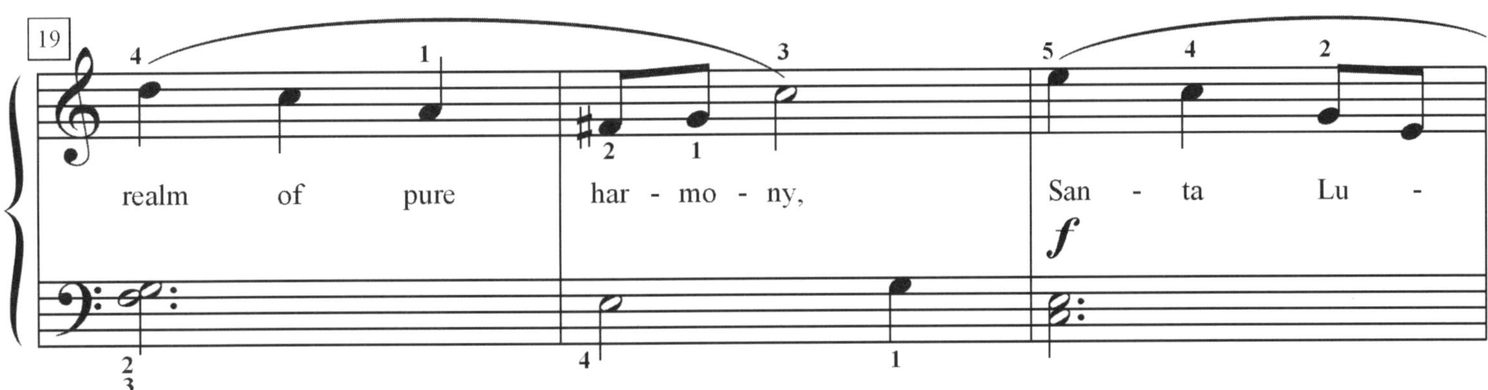

19
4 1 3 5 4 2
realm of pure har - mo - ny, San - ta Lu -
2 1 f
4 1
2
3

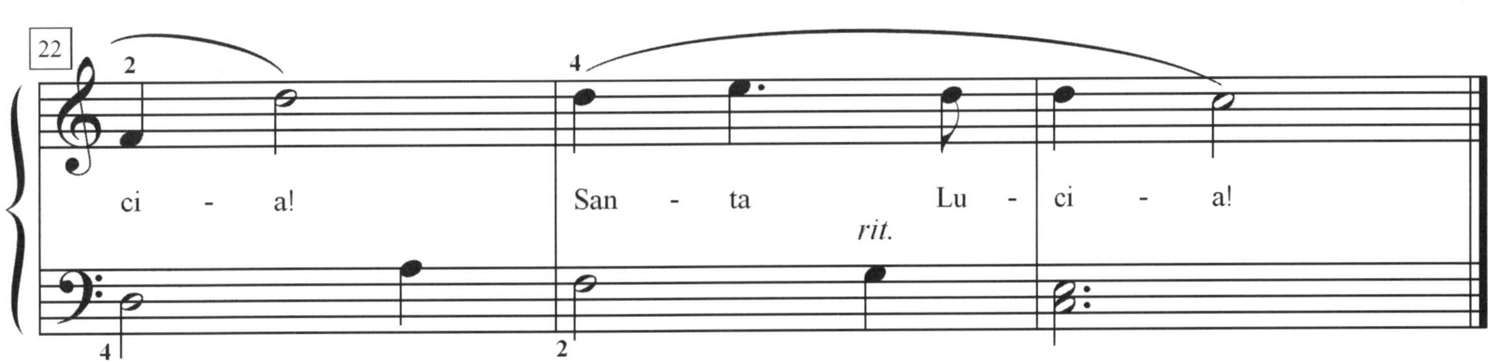

22
2 4
ci - a! San - ta Lu - ci - a!
rit.
4 2

Mattinata

Con passione ♩ = 112-120
Ruggiero Leoncavallo
Words by C. E. Cook
Let's walk in the gar - den of dreams, dear, the
mys - ti - cal gar - den of dreams. Where
thoughts are the on - ly things real, dear, the
world is al - most what it seems.
p
mp
mf

All is se - rene, here in love's gar - den,
mp
e - ter - nal spring, where hap - pi - ness beams.
rit.
Noth - ing shall with - er, while we are there, dear.
f a tempo
Wish that our dream world could some day be real.
rit.
mp

O Sole Mio*

Eduardo di Capua
Words by John W. Schaum

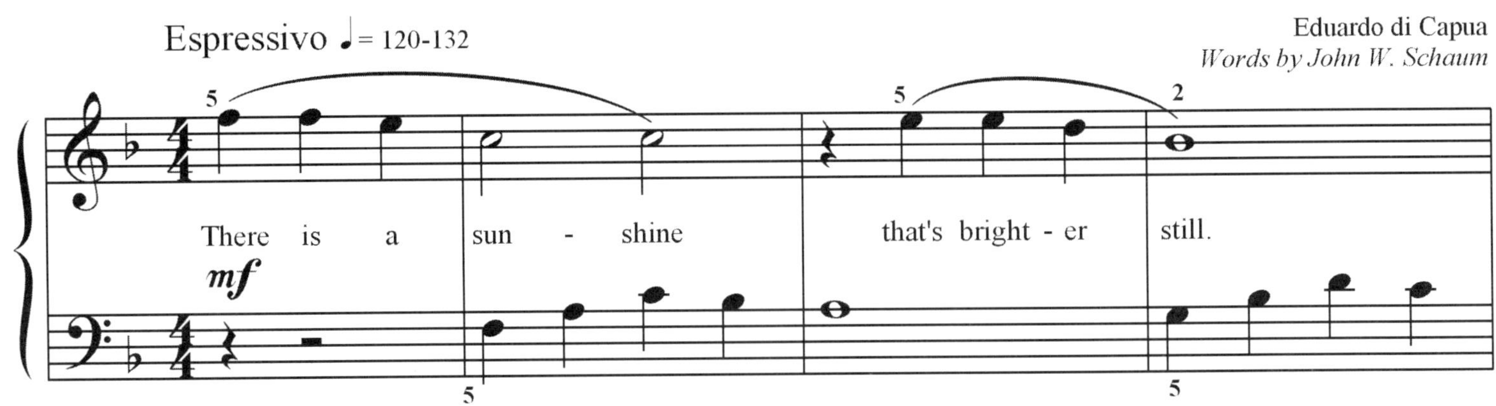

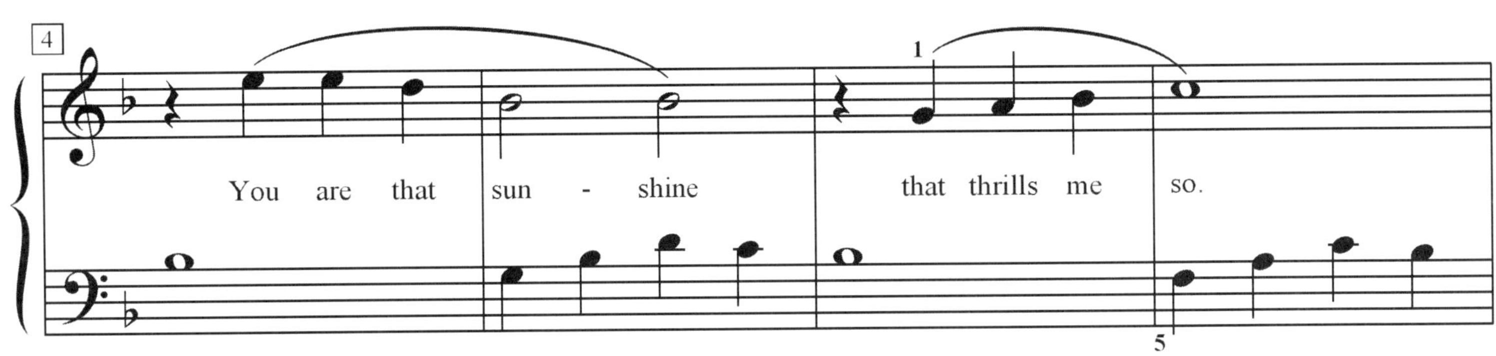

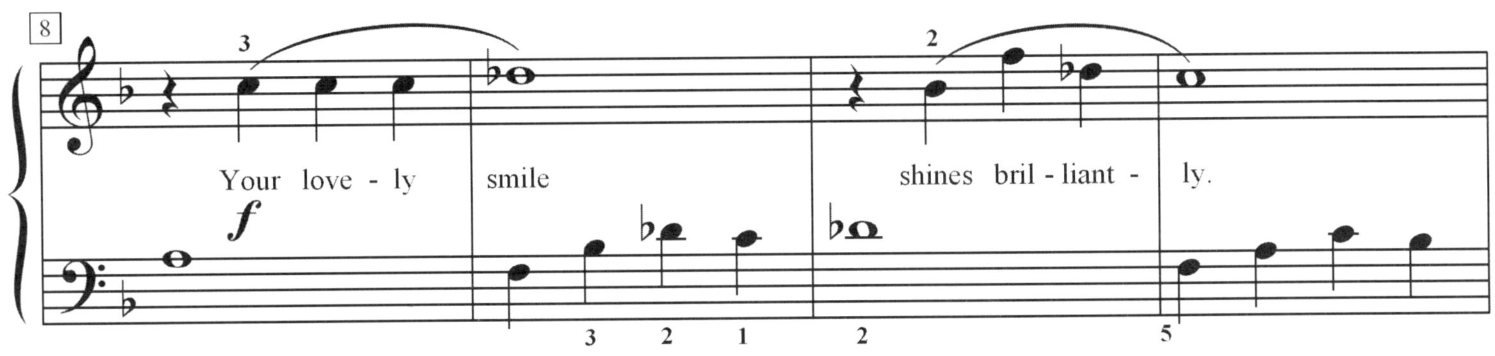

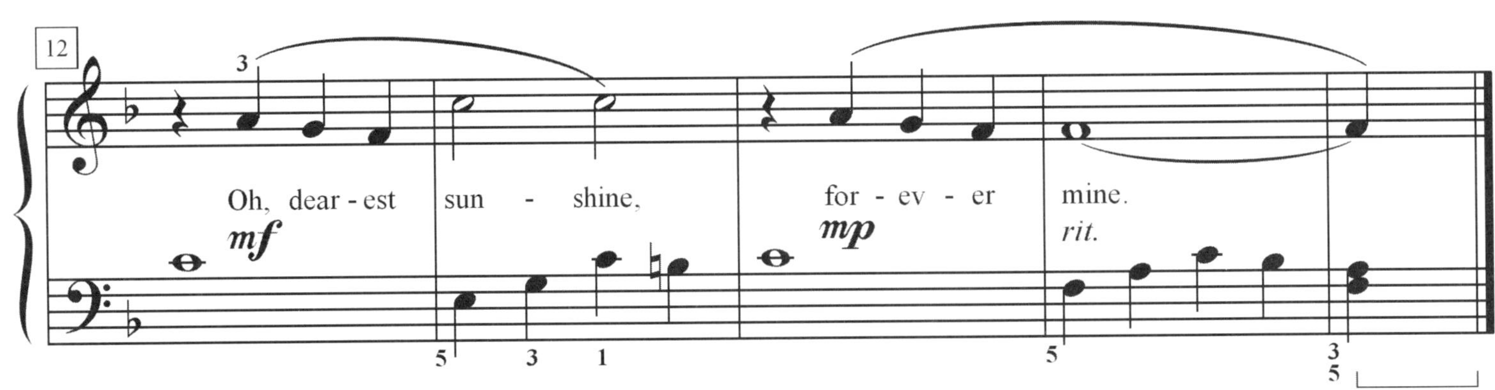

* *O Sole Mio* means "my sunshine."

Carnival of Venice

Folk Song
Words by John W. Schaum

Serenade

Come Back to Sorrento